Piano_Trainer Series_

The Intermediate Pianist Book 3

Karen Marshall & Heather Hammond

Contents

Introduction

Moving a student successfully and positively on to the intermediate levels (Grades 3 – 5) can be a tricky process. At this stage, it takes too long to learn music by rote, so **well-developed note-reading skills** are key. Students also need to have a **good understanding of style** – they can no longer simply play music the way they think it should sound to give a convincing performance. Finally, **sound technique** and **good theoretical knowledge** are required to tackle trickier repertoire. *The Intermediate Pianist* books provide a one-stop shop for building all these skills.

The material is organised into chapters that are designed to give approximately one month's work. Each chapter contains a variety of elements as described below. The music deliberately spans a range of difficulty levels, so some pieces can be learnt in just one or two weeks, whilst others are more challenging. The terms used throughout also support and reflect those required for GCSE Music.

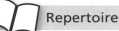 **Quick learn**   At least a grade below the ability level, these pieces and studies consolidate skills, maintain interest and improve note reading.

 **Repertoire**   Specially selected pieces give excellent experience of the style in each chapter.

Technique   Exercises and activities to develop the key technical skills required.

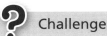 **Challenge**   Imaginative ideas to deepen musical understanding and knowledge.

Activities   Things to do to prepare for the pieces and develop musicianship.

 Theory   A range of exercises to improve theory alongside playing ability.

 Recital pieces   Stand-alone pieces perfect for performances, unconnected to the style of the chapter.

We hope you find *The Intermediate Pianist* a journey of discovery that brings a love of music from many different periods and styles.

Happy music making!

Karen Marshall and Heather Hammond

Getting started

Activity   Included in this piece are all the styles explored in the book.
Listen to your teacher play it: what do you notice about each style?

What Shall We Do with the Drunken Sailor?

Traditional arr. Heather Hammond

Riffs and ostinato

A **riff** is a short repeated melody or chord sequence commonly used in pop and jazz music.

The word '**ostinato**' is thought to come from the Italian for 'stubborn' and the Latin 'obstinate'. It is used to describe a repeated rhythm, phrase or pattern of notes in Classical music.

Challenge

Listen to Ravel's *Bolero* then try to play the ostinato bass line by ear.

Quick learn

A Major Riff

Karen Marshall

Activity

Try playing *A Major Riff* in A minor – and then in another major key.

Write your own riff – a pattern of notes which works well when you repeat it.

Modes

Modes are very old scales that originated from sacred music. They are useful to improvise with and to play over ostinato bass lines. These are the seven modes – each starts on a different note and uses only the white notes. That means each mode has a different pattern of tones and semitones. Can you mark in the semitones between the notes of each scale below?

Ionion (major scale)	C	D	E	F	G	A	B	C
Dorian	D	E	F	G	A	B	C	D
Phrygian	E	F	G	A	B	C	D	E
Lydian	F	G	A	B	C	D	E	F
Mixolydian	G	A	B	C	D	E	F	G
Aeolian (natural minor)	A	B	C	D	E	F	G	A
Locrian	B	C	D	E	F	G	A	B

Here's a rhyme to remember the names of the modes in order:
I Don't **P**lay **L**ike **M**iles **A**fter **L**unch.

You can form a mode on any note using the same patterns of tones and semitones. So an Aeolian mode on E would be E F♯ G A B C D E.

 Activity

Using the perfect fifth intervals of D–A and C–G, create your own ostinato accompaniment to *Drunken Sailor*, which is in the Dorian mode.

Drunken Sailor Improvisation

Traditional

 Activity Can you identify the ostinato in the bass? What are the intervals of each chord?

 Quick learn

The Italian Bagpipers

Charles Gounod

2 Latin dance styles

Challenge

Find videos of all the dances below, then come up with a describing word for each to go with the music. Here are some ideas:

Fast   Dramatic   Flowing   Spiky   Crisp   Rhythmic

A **tango** is a dance from Argentina that originated in the early 1800s. Usually written in $\frac{2}{4}$ or $\frac{4}{4}$, often with dotted rhythms, tangos are commonly in a minor key.

Describing word _____

Rumba originated in Cuba in the 1930s and features complicated rhythms. The word rumba has been used in Cuba to mean 'party'. Accents often appear on the first, fourth and seventh of eight quavers.

Here is a rumba-style rhythm. Can you clap it on your knees: the top line on your right knee and the bottom line on your left?

Describing word _____

A **samba** is a Brazilian dance which is believed to have originated in Africa. It is usually in two time and features syncopated rhythms.

Describing word _____

Bossa nova (meaning 'new trend') is another Brazilian dance, believed to have derived from the samba, but with a greater emphasis on melody.

Describing word _____

Cha cha cha is a popular Cuban dance that emerged in the 1950s. The name cha cha cha comes from the rhythm of the dancers' feet.

Describing word _____

Clap the right-hand rhythm of bars 8–11.

Repertoire

Blue-sky Bossa

Heather Hammond

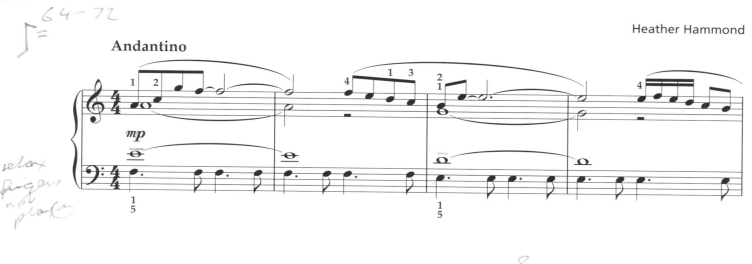

Andantino

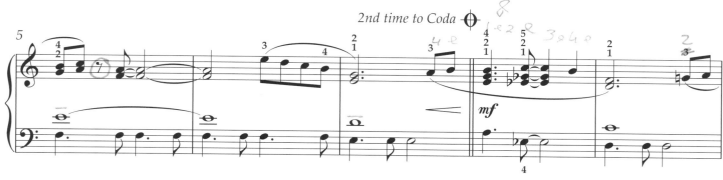

2nd time to Coda

mf

D.C. al Coda

f

dim.

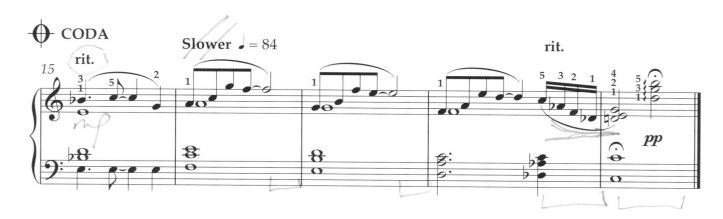

CODA
rit.

Slower ♩ = 84

rit.

pp

 Activity

Circle all the changes in time signature and describe them (e.g. $\frac{4}{4}$ is simple quadruple time). How is this piece different to a traditional rumba?

 Repertoire

Rumba Rhythmique

Heather Hammond

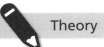
Theory

Augmented and diminished intervals

- If a major or perfect interval is made larger by one semitone, it becomes **augmented**.
- If a major interval is made smaller by one semitone it becomes minor.
- If a minor or perfect interval becomes smaller by one semitone it becomes **diminished**.

Activity

Try to identify these intervals:

Activity   Can you find an augmented fourth interval in the fifth line? Bar _____

Repertoire

Samba

Heather Hammond

Keys with five sharps and flats

Can you work out the notes of the D flat major scale and its relative minor, B♭ minor? Highlight them on the keyboards below, along with the fingering that you think works best.

D♭ major

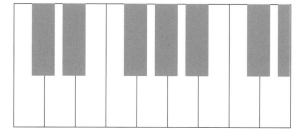

B♭ harmonic minor

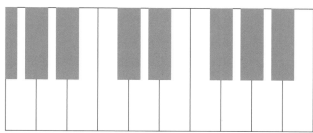

Then fill in the blanks for the arpeggios:

D♭ [ ] A♭ [ ]   B♭ D♭ [ ] [ ]

Can you work out the notes of the B major scale and its relative minor, G♯ minor? Highlight them on the keyboards below, along with the fingering that you think works best. Note that G♯ minor needs a double sharp (raising a note by two semitones). It looks like this: 𝄪

B major

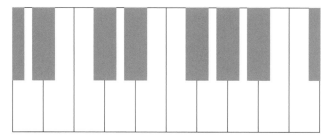

G♯ harmonic minor

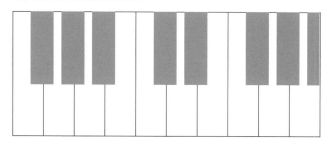

Then fill in the blanks for the arpeggios:

B [ ] F♯ [ ]   G♯ B [ ] [ ]

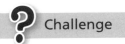

Challenge

Can you transpose the first three bars of the right hand into C major?
You need to start on a G (up a perfect fifth), and the E♭ will become a B♭.

Quick learn

Summer Cha-cha

Heather Hammond

Theme and variations was a particularly popular form during the Baroque period (1600–1750), and also during the Classical period (1750–1820) and beyond. The main idea, the theme, is presented several times but is varied and developed using different accompaniments, rhythms and so on.

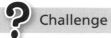 Challenge

Listen to Handel's Passacaglia in G minor (the orchestral version). This is a Baroque theme and variations, although it's called a *passacaglia* (which is one of the less common movements in a Baroque dance suite). Then listen to Mozart's Twelve Variations on *Ah vous dirai-je, Maman*, K.265 for piano. This is a theme and variations written in the Classical period.

Compare the two pieces and state the similarities and differences:

	Similarities	Differences
Baroque Theme and Variations		
Classical Theme and Variations		

 Theory

The Classical orchestra was different to the Baroque orchestra. Work out the following anagrams of the instruments in the orchestra – the asterisks indicate instruments that were new in the classical orchestra.

LETUF _____

EBOO _____

TENRICAL* _____

OBONASS* _____

RUPMETT* _____

NAPIMIT* _____

STRIF NIVOLI _____

SCONED LOVINI _____

OLAVI _____

LOCEL _____

OBULED SABS* _____

CHRENF RONH _____

A Chaconne is a slow, stately Baroque dance, usually in triple time.
It often featured variations based on a repeated harmonic progression.
Add your own dynamics and phrasing here.

Repertoire

Chaconne
(Selected variations)

George Frideric Handel

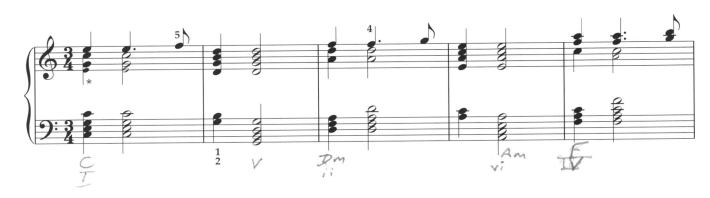

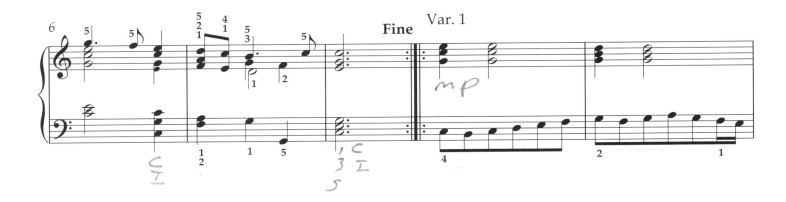

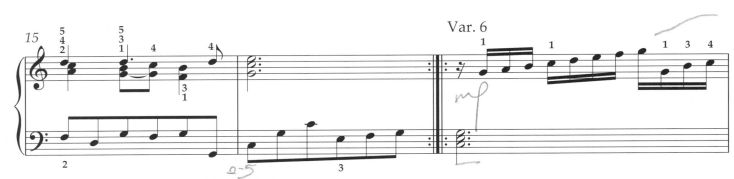

* Cue-sized notes may be omitted by smaller hands.

Var. 11 (adapted)

 Theory

Exploring different bass lines

Play this chord sequence from the Chaconne:

C   G   D minor   A minor   F   C   F   G   C

Here are two variations on this chord sequence. Can you sight-read them?

1 Alberti bass

2 Arpeggio patterns

 Challenge

Compose your own Chaconne variation

Make up your own bass line, based on the chord sequence above. Then add a melody for the right hand and play your new variation.

Activity

Can you mark in the chords at the cadences in this piece? The first has been done for you and the boxes show where they are.

What is the form of the piece? _____

Recital piece

Andantino

Joseph Haydn

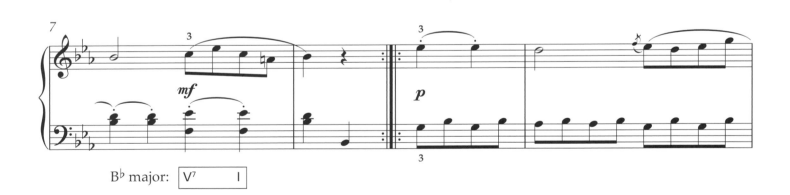

B♭ major: | V⁷ | I |

E♭ major:

E♭ major:

Dominant and diminished sevenths

A **dominant seventh** starts on the fifth note of the key and the chord is built up of the first, third, fifth and seventh notes. Play this C major arpeggio, then play it again with an added B♭. This turns it into a dominant seventh in F.

Fill in the missing notes for these dominant seventh chords:

Dominant seventh in the key of C

G ☐ ☐ F

Dominant seventh in the key of G

☐ F♯ ☐ C

A **diminished seventh** is made up of minor third intervals. You can start a diminished seventh on any note. Here are diminished sevenths on C and D. Finger patterns for dominant and diminished sevenths always use every finger. The starting finger depends on the position of the black notes.

Flat-key Study

Remember, in D♭ major the only white keys are F and C.

Heather Hammond

4 Music for television, film and music theatre

Music is an essential element of television, film and music theatre, creating atmosphere, emotion and interest for the audience.

The pieces below have featured on television and in adverts. Listen to both and fill in their key features. Finally, find out where each has been used.

1 'Dance of the Knights' from _Romeo and Juliet_ (Sergei Prokofiev)

Describe the melody and harmony. _____

Describe the rhythm, time signature and tempo. _____

What is the tonality and structure? _____

Describe the sonority. _____

Describe the texture. _____

Describe the dynamics. _____

2 'O Fortuna' from _Carmina Burana_ (Carl Orff)

Describe the melody and harmony. _____

Describe the rhythm, time signature and tempo. _____

What is the tonality and structure? _____

Describe the sonority. _____

Describe the texture. _____

Describe the dynamics. _____

Melody Can move in steps (conjunct) or leaps (disjunct), or feature patterns or scales.

Harmony What is the chord structure? Is it diatonic? Cadences?

Rhythm, time signature and tempo Look out for features such as syncopation, dotted rhythms and simple or compound time.

Tonality Major or minor – or possibly modal or atonal (without key).

Structure Such as binary (A B), ternary (A B A), rondo (A B A C A) or theme and variations, etc.

Sonority The orchestration, articulation (staccato, legato, accents) and timbre (type of sound).

Texture Monophonic (one line), homophonic (several parts moving together) or polyphonic (different parts moving independently).

Dynamics Loud (_forte_), quiet (_piano_), getting louder (_crescendo_) and getting quieter (_decrescendo_).

Activity

Listen to this song before you play it – it was written for two singers, a soprano and an alto. Remember, in B major the only white notes are B and E.

Repertoire

The Flower Duet

From *Lakmé*

Léo Delibes
Arr. Heather Hammond

This music was used at the very end of the film *The King's Speech*, when
King George VI addressed the nation.

Recital piece

Allegretto

From Symphony No.7

Ludwig van Beethoven
Arr. Heather Hammond

 Quick learn

Don't Dilly Dally

My Old Man

Traditional
Arr. Heather Hammond

5 Mazurkas and Romanticism

A **mazurka** is a Polish dance in three time that features dotted rhythms and an accented second beat. Mazurkas were popular during the Romantic period – Chopin in particular composed many.

The Romantic period (1800–1900)

The piano develops In the Romantic period, pianos began to have metal rather than wooden frames. Their strings became longer and the hammers were covered in felt rather than leather, all of which produced a better tone. The keyboard extended to over seven octaves and pedals were added: the sustain pedal holds on the notes and the *una corda* pedal reduces the volume. After these developments the piano had more dynamic range and became a popular instrument for Romantic composers.

Music becomes more dramatic Artists and writers became much more expressive in their work: literature explored the deepest of emotions – pain, grief, love and joy. Artists depicted the extremities of human life and also the beauty of nature. Composers were influenced by the artists and writers of the time and music became more dramatic and evocative. Orchestras became bigger, with more percussion, woodwind and brass. Brass instruments developed a much wider note range as they now had valves.

Challenge Listen to these famous Romantic works: *Peer Gynt* Suite No.1 (Edvard Grieg) and *Rhapsody on a Theme of Paganini* (Sergei Rachmaninoff).

Activity **Romantic period wordsearch**

F	B	G	M	P	B	K	U	T	J
L	I	E	D	E	R	N	E	S	R
I	L	D	B	R	A	H	M	S	P
S	R	H	E	C	S	F	G	E	Q
Z	C	L	A	U	S	D	M	V	H
T	W	J	R	S	C	N	I	L	P
J	S	K	E	S	E	G	R	A	L
C	H	O	P	I	N	V	O	V	Z
I	P	W	O	O	D	W	I	N	D
T	K	H	G	N	X	L	F	M	N

OPERA

LIEDER

CHOPIN

BRAHMS

LISZT

BRASS

VALVES

LARGE

PERCUSSION

WOODWIND

Activity

Listen to this and some of the other pieces in Tchaikovsky's *Children's Album*.

Repertoire

Mazurka

From *Children's Album* Op.39

Pyotr Ilyich Tchaikovsky

Tempo di Mazurka

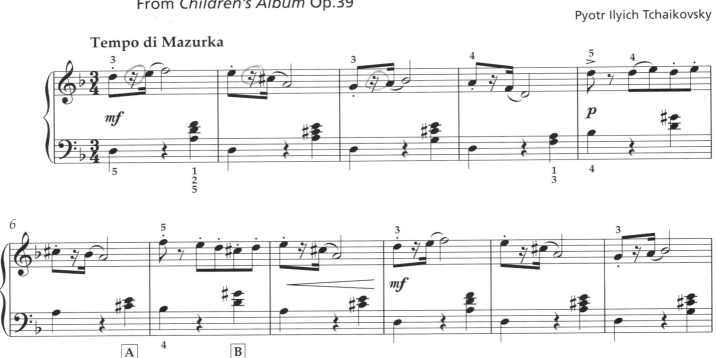

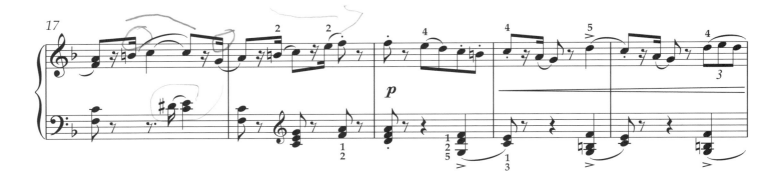

Theory

Can you identify the harmonic intervals in the music?

A _____

B _____

C _____

D _____

E _____

Technique   Take great care with the pauses in this duet, decide in advance with your duet partner how long you will hold them.

Recital piece

Gypsy Serenade Duet

Secondo

Heather Hammond

Gypsy Serenade Duet

Primo

Heather Hammond

6 Exploring impressionism

Impressionism drew its name from a style of painting that developed around the end of the 19th century among artists such as Monet, Renoir and Pissarro, whose work created an overall impression rather than focusing on the detail of a scene. Composers such as Debussy, Ravel and Satie were inspired by these painters, composing light, atmospheric compositions that were often influenced by nature. Their music extended the boundaries of traditional classical harmonies and structures.

Challenge

Listen to 'Sarabande' from *Pour la piano*, *La fille aux cheveux de lin* and *Clair de lune* by Debussy. Sight-read the extracts below from these pieces.

1 Sarabande from *Pour La Piano* left hand only. Notice the modal chords.

Avec une elegance grave et lente

2 La fille aux cheveux de lin (*The girl with the flaxen hair*), right hand only. Notice the haunting, pentatonic melody and key signature.

Tres calme et doucement expressif ($\bullet = 66$)

3 Clair de lune. Notice the arpeggio figures and adventurous harmony.

Tempo rubato

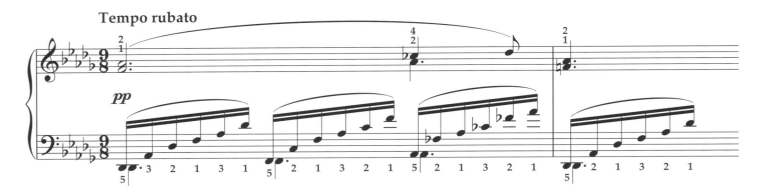

Challenge

This piece is written in the Dorian mode (see page 7).
Can you play a two-octave scale in the Dorian mode?

 Quick learn

Dorian's Dance

Heather Hammond

With an air of mystery

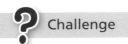 **Challenge** Point out some features that make this piece impressionistic.
Can you add some pedal marks?

 **Repertoire**

Gymnopédie No. 3

Erik Satie

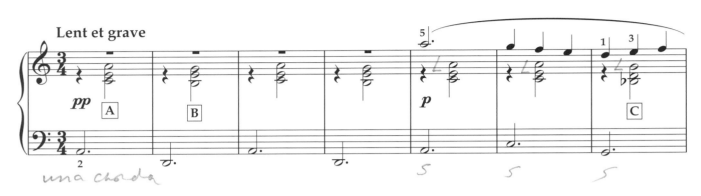

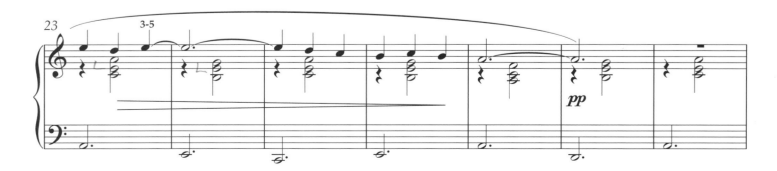

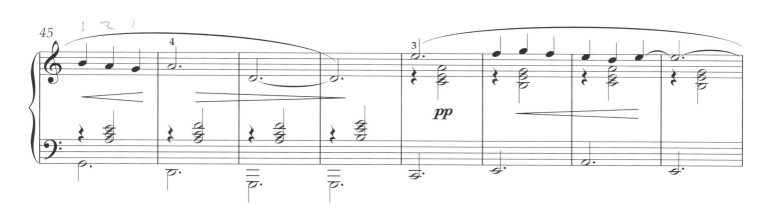

 Theory   Can you identify the triads that are labelled A–F?

_____

_____

Looking at minimalism

Like impressionism, **minimalism** takes its names from art – minimalist paintings often feature simple shapes, solid colours and little detail. Minimalist music is similarly pared back and simple, and usually based on small motifs and short repeated patterns that change very gradually.

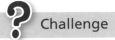 Challenge

Listen to Philip Glass' *Metamorphosis Two* for piano. How is this minimalistic?

Listen to Steve Reich's *New York Counterpoint* for clarinet. How do you think it reflects the New York skyline? Try to find out how the soloist plays all seven parts.

Sight-read these minimalistic motifs. Can you work out what compositional technique has been used to change the original motif each time?*

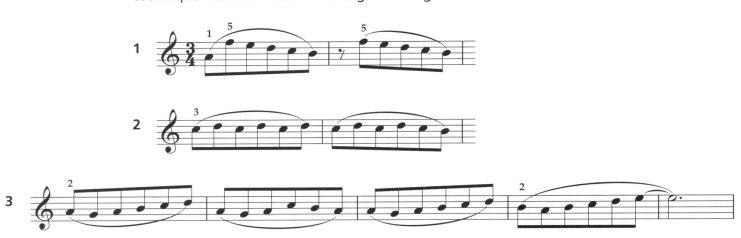

 Activity

20th-century period wordsearch

E	N	O	H	P	O	X	A	S	I	D	O	J
W	X	Z	J	P	F	R	E	E	F	O	R	M
A	W	P	Q	I	P	H	N	G	M	R	U	K
T	U	V	R	T	S	O	B	R	C	S	S	F
O	U	X	K	E	L	O	O	P	I	N	G	H
N	Y	E	W	L	S	N	H	C	S	P	J	G
A	B	F	U	V	M	S	A	O	T	I	R	Y
L	S	E	R	I	A	L	I	S	M	S	R	E
A	X	C	F	G	S	U	T	O	D	Z	P	K
J	A	Z	Z	H	A	R	M	O	N	Y	M	O
A	R	T	S	E	H	C	R	O	G	I	B	N
C	A	B	E	G	N	I	L	P	M	A	S	A
D	E	L	E	C	T	R	O	N	I	C	B	M

EXPRESSIONISM

SERIALISM

BIG ORCHESTRA

ATONAL

JAZZ HARMONY

FREEFORM

MUSICALS

ELECTRONIC

SAXOPHONE

LOOPING

SAMPLING

Answers
1 Use of rests.
2 Notes added or taken away.
3 Intervals slightly alter.

Chords, cadences and figured bass

Figured bass is a way of indicating harmony without writing out the chords over a bass line. Numbers indicate the intervals of the notes over the bass note.

$\frac{5}{3}$ Indicates a triad built on the bottom note (the **root**) of the chord.
In figured bass if no number appears then you assume it is this chord.

$\frac{6}{3}$ This indicates a **first inversion chord** – the bottom note is the 3rd of the chord.
The other two notes of the chord are a 3rd and 6th above this.
This is usually shown as just a 6, with the 3 missing.

$\frac{6}{4}$ This is a **second inversion chord** – the bottom note is the 5th of the chord.
The other two notes of the chord are a 4th and 6th above this.

7 If just a 7 appears, the seventh note above the bass note is included.

Apart from the bottom note, any configuration of the other notes between the hands is allowed.

Here is a series of chords, with their chord names and roman numeral descriptions.

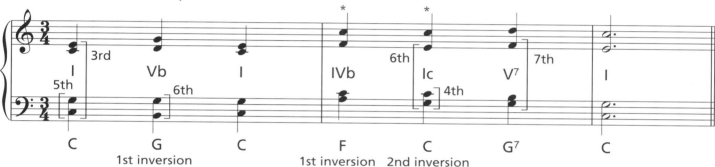

Here is the same chord sequence indicated by figured bass. Can you 'realise' it (write in the harmony)?

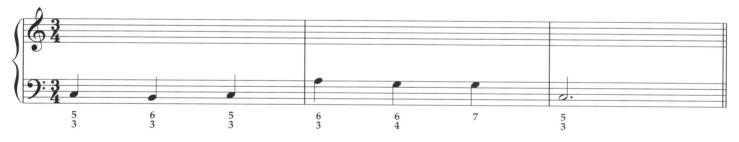

The cadential $\frac{6}{4}$ progression

A $\frac{6}{4}$ $\frac{5}{3}$ chord progression is often used at cadence points. It is called a **cadential 6/4** and indicates chords Ic–V. Note that the bass note stays the same. Have a look at it in *Happy Birthday*.

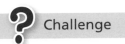 **Challenge** — What are the features of this piece that make it minimalist?

 **Repertoire**

Nuovi Inizi Dedicated to Emily W.
New Beginnings

Karen Marshall

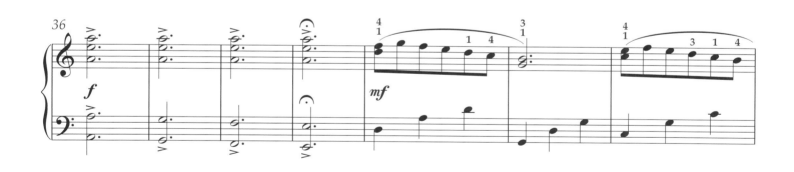

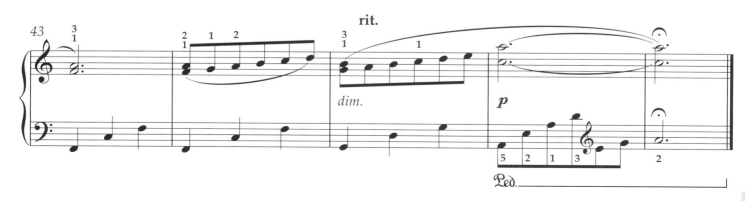

 **Activity**

This piece is from the Baroque period but, like minimalist music, it also uses a melodic motif. Can you identify it? Remember, Baroque music was generally written without any markings, so you should add your own. See page 50 for more information about ornaments.

 Recital piece

Two-part Invention

Johann Sebastian Bach

8 Introducing fugues

A **fugue** is formed from a melodic idea which is introduced in one part, then played by one or more other parts entering at different times. Fugues were most popular during the Baroque period. Here are the terms used to describe the elements in a fugue.

> **Subject** The melody (or theme) introduced by the first part.
>
> **Answer** A response to the subject, often in the dominant or sub-dominant key (the fifth or fourth notes of the scale) which seems to 'answer' the theme. It is usually in the second part.
>
> **Countersubject** A second subject (or melody) which often accompanies the original subject or its answer.
>
> **Exposition** The opening section, which incorporates all the parts entering and stating the subject and answer.
>
> **Modulation section** The subject is transposed into different keys in this section.
>
> **Final section (or recapitulation)** The subject returns in the original key to bring the fugue to a close.
>
> **Stretto** An overlapping of subject entries. This often occurs towards the end, heightening the tension before the climax.
>
> **Augmentation and diminution** Lengthening or shortening of the notes of the subject.
>
> **Episode** A section avoiding the use of the subject.

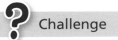

Challenge

Listen to a piano fugue by J.S. Bach. Which words do you think about when you listen to it?

Theory

A **modulation** is where a piece of music moves to a different key. Fugues often modulate, as do many other musical forms. Modulations are usually to a related key: the relative major/minor, the dominant and sub-dominant and their relative majors/minors.

Have a look at the fugue on page 48. Can you identify the modulations in the music? All the key changes are listed below – you just need to add in their relationships to the key of the piece.

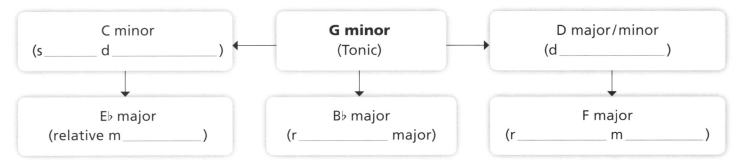

C minor	G minor	D major/minor
(s_____ d_____)	(Tonic)	(d_____)

E♭ major	B♭ major	F major
(relative m_____)	(r_____ major)	(r_____ m_____)

Quick learn

Frugal Fugue

Karen Marshall &
Heather Hammond

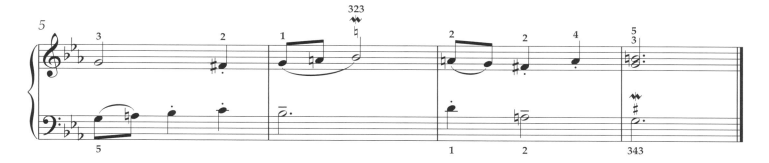

Activity

Fugue wordsearch

Can you find the terms used in a fugue?

E	M	A	L	O	R	H	M	I	D	M	T
N	X	B	C	P	S	U	M	V	I	G	C
A	K	P	T	N	H	O	K	G	M	F	E
B	A	R	O	Q	U	E	N	M	I	O	J
M	L	R	T	S	R	S	P	F	N	U	B
E	W	E	T	P	I	X	O	E	U	L	U
P	R	W	E	D	E	T	B	Z	T	K	S
T	U	S	R	E	C	D	I	H	I	R	R
W	E	N	T	R	I	E	S	O	O	J	E
S	O	A	S	E	D	S	F	G	N	B	T
A	U	G	M	E	N	T	A	T	I	O	N
R	S	Q	E	B	O	D	F	R	A	R	U
S	G	P	T	C	E	J	B	U	S	S	O
A	P	R	S	O	R	G	H	D	B	A	C

SUBJECT

ANSWER

COUNTERSUBJECT

EXPOSITION

STRETTO

AUGMENTATION

DIMINUTION

BAROQUE

ENTRIES

 **Challenge**   Can you find the subject and answer in the music?

 **Repertoire**   # Fugue in G minor

Georg Philipp Telemann

9 All about ornaments

Ornaments are symbols that tell you to play certain patterns of notes without the notes being written out in full. Here are all the most common ornaments, with their names and signs.

Turn ∽ ⌇

This ornament 'turns around' the original note. A line through the symbol indicates the notes are played the other way round (starting below the note).

Trill *tr*

There are lots of ways to play trills. They often end with a turn.

Mordent ⌁ ⌁

Moves to the note above and back again. A line through the symbol indicates the mordent goes down rather than up.

Appoggiatura ♩

This is also known as a grace note. It takes half the length of the main note. When the main note is dotted, the appoggiatura takes two-thirds of the beat.

Acciaccatura ♩

Also known as a crushed note, this is so short it is 'crushed' against the main note.

Arpeggiated chord

This means the chord is broken into an ascending or descending arpeggio, with all the notes being held on once played.

♫ Technique

Exercise No. 23 Extract

From *101 Exercises for Piano*

For playing *legato* two-part chords – use the suggested fingering to make sure you keep a good *legato* sound.

Carl Czerny

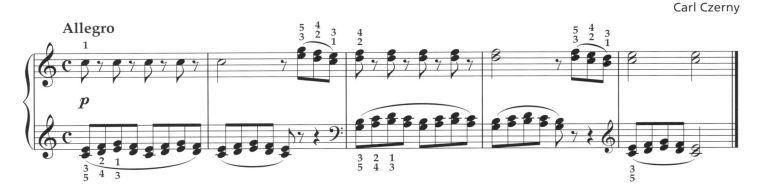

 **Activity**

Each of the ornaments on page 50 are included in this study. Write the correct ornament sign above each (written out) ornament in the box provided.

Ornament Olympics Version 1

Heather Hammond

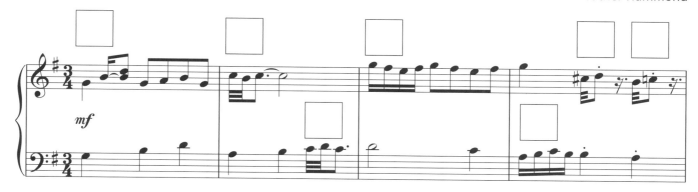

⚡ **Quick learn**

Ornament Olympics Version 2

Now play this study with the ornaments.

Heather Hammond

Exercise No. 14

From *101 Exercises for Piano*

Carl Czerny

 Theory

Can you identify the intervals, chords and cadences marked A to E in the music?

 Recital piece

Spinning Song

Albert Ellmenreich

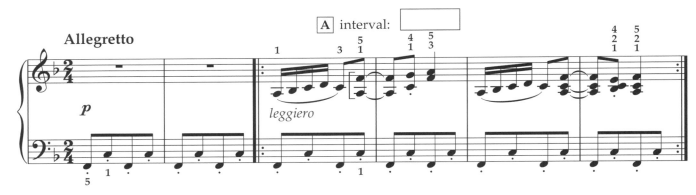

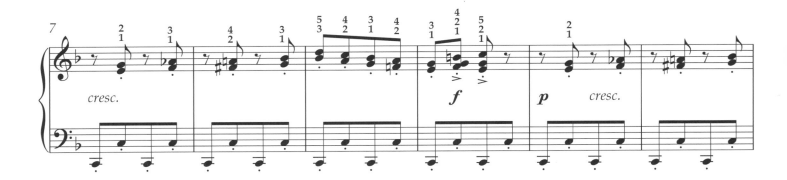

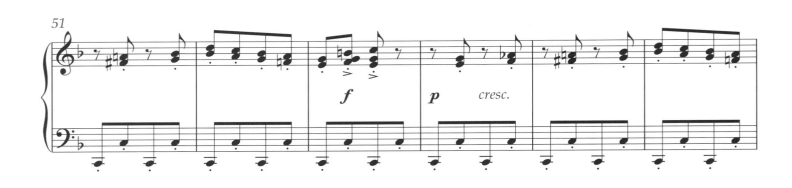

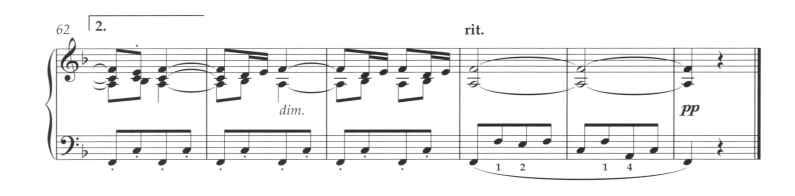

(10) Concert pieces

This section gives you a selection of pieces from different styles and periods to play now that you've completed this book. Try the activities on this page with every piece – you can photocopy this page if you like.

Name of piece _____

☐ Clap the pulse as your teacher plays the piece, stressing the first beat of each bar.

☐ Is it in 2, 3 or 4 time – or another time signature?

_____

☐ Your teacher will play two bars from the piece – sing the melody back. (NB teachers can transpose the melody into singing range as needed.)

☐ Describe the style/period of the music. _____

☐ What are the dynamics? _____

☐ How would you describe the tempo? (Use an Italian term if you can.) _____

☐ Is the piece in a major or minor key (or both)?

_____

☐ Your teacher will play a bar and then play it again with a change to the pitch or rhythm. What is the change?

_____

☐ Your teacher will play an interval from the piece (either a 2nd, 3rd, perfect 4th, 5th or octave). Name the interval.

_____

☐ Circle the correct description for the time signature of the piece:

Simple duple   Compound duple
Simple triple   Compound triple
Simple quadruple   Compound quadruple

☐ Find out three facts about the composer:

_____

_____

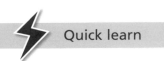

La Bourbonnaise

(Baroque)

François Couperin

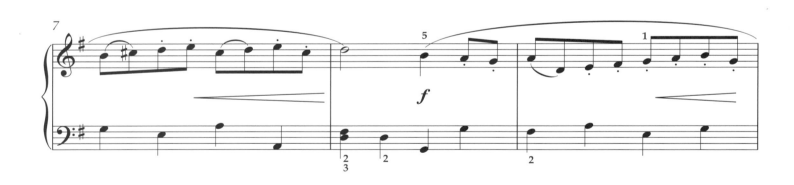

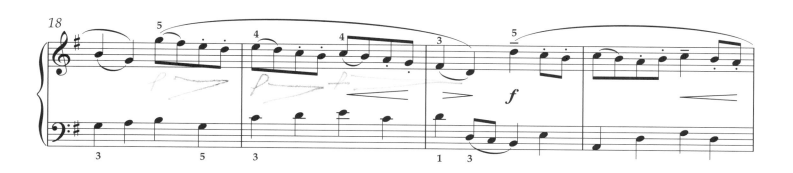

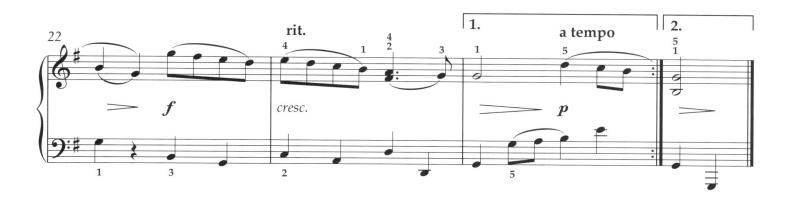

Theory

1 Explain the time signature and key signature. _____

_____

2 Can you spot any sequences (the same pattern starting on a different note)
   in the music?

3 In which bar does the music modulate to D major? _____

The Fall of the Leafe

From *The Fitzwilliam Virginal Book*

(Renaissance)

Martin Peerson

How to play the ornaments:

Theory

1 What is the name of the chord in the first bar? _____

2 What type of ornament is most common in this piece? _____

3 This piece uses 'word painting'. How is bar 11 linked to the title?

_____

Quick learn

Allegretto

(Classical)

Wolfgang Amadeus Mozart

Theory

1 Which bars include syncopated rhythms? _____

2 Where are the appoggiaturas? _____

3 Which interval is most common in the left hand of this piece? _____

Prelude in C minor

Op.28 No.20

(Romantic)

Frédéric Chopin

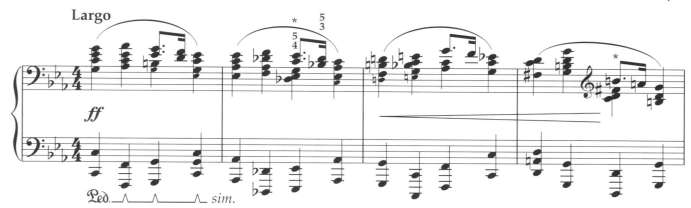

* These chords can be split if the span is too great.
Cue-sized notes can be omitted as well to help smaller hands.

Theory

1 Can you identify the first two chords? _____

2 Where does the music modulate to G major? _____

 Quick learn

Summer Jazz Waltz

(Contemporary)

Heather Hammond

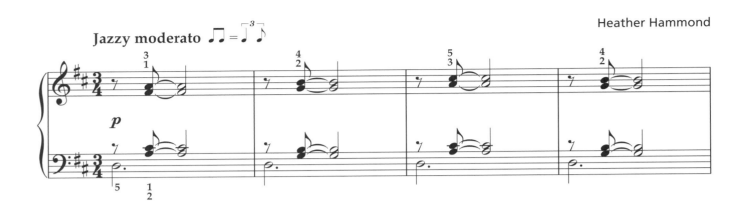

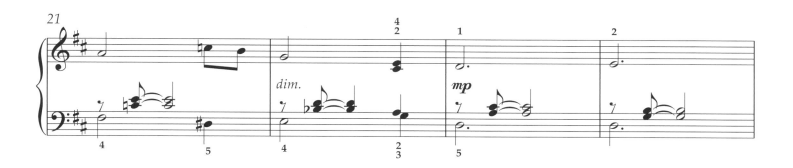

Theory

1 How do you know this piece uses swung quavers (eighth notes)?

_____

2 Can you find a harmonic interval of a minor third and an augmented fourth in the piece?

_____

3 Look at bars 20–21. What is the interval between E♯ and F♯? _____

We greatly appreciate all the feedback on the books we have received from many very gifted piano teachers. We have listened to you all! Lindsey Berwin, Barbara Bury, Andrew Dunlop, Andrew Eales, Helen Marshall, Matthew Palmer, Jo Peach, Julian Saphir, Penny Stirling, Jean White. Huge thanks also to Faber Music and Lesley Rutherford (our editor).

Dedicated to Christopher Johnson (CJ), Karen's secondary school music teacher. Your inspiring, accessible and creative teaching has been a blueprint for my own career. Huge thanks!

Answers are available on the product page on fabermusicstore.com

© 2017 by Faber Music Ltd
This edition first published in 2017
Bloomsbury House, 74–77 Great Russell Street, London WC1B 3DA
Music processed by Jackie Leigh
Text designed by Susan Clarke
Cover design by adamhaystudio.com
Printed in England by Caligraving Ltd
All rights reserved

ISBN10: 0-571-54003-1
EAN13: 978-0-571-54003-7

To buy Faber Music publications or to find out about the full range of titles available please contact your local music retailer or Faber Music sales enquiries:
Faber Music Ltd, Burnt Mill, Elizabeth Way, Harlow CM20 2HX
Tel: +44 (0) 1279 82 89 82   Fax: +44 (0) 1279 82 89 83
sales@fabermusic.com   fabermusicstore.com